Leptin Resistance

(Get Healthy Now)

How to get permanent weight loss, cure obesity, control your hormones, and live healthy

Table of Contents

Introduction

Leptin is one of the most vital hormones in the body. It plays a crucial role in regulating body fats. Poor leptin levels can cause you to deal with a number of weight-related issues including obesity and being overweight. These issues can further lead to more severe health conditions. This is the main reason why you have to correct poor leptin levels in the body.

Since leptin plays a major role in fat regulation, appetite suppression and the feelings of fullness, many researchers are looking into it as a potential weight loss or anti-obesity solution. Note that this vital hormone is capable of controlling a lot more areas in your body aside from your feelings of fullness.

However, you cannot just allow your leptin levels to go excessively high. The problem is that your body consistently tries to make some adjustments on its basal leptin levels. This means that if you consistently supply your body with it, especially if you are either overweight or obese, then there is a great possibility for your brain to lose its sensitivity to the hormone.

Supplying your body with excessive amounts of leptin, to the point that it already goes beyond normal maintenance levels, can trigger leptin resistance. If you have this condition, then your body will no longer be able to determine if the stored fats are already too high. It can also desensitize leptin receptors. The more your body resists leptin, the harder it will be to regulate fat so staying lean will also become a problem.

Considering the way leptin works, it is no longer surprising to see people who view it as an enemy. The good news is that this book "Leptin Resistance" is now around to guide you in the process of understanding leptin and the specific way it works, so you can maintain healthy levels of this hormone (not too high and not too low).

This book also covers a number of vital topics such as the nature of leptin resistance, its main causes and symptoms. You will also know a few signs that will help you determine if you are already resistant to the hormone. The good thing about this book is that it also extensively covers a number of potential solutions for leptin resistance. You will learn how to handle the problem through diet and lifestyle changes. Expect to have an easier time changing your diet with the recipes covered in this book.

The book will also talk about supplements and alternative medicines for the condition. With the aid of this book, you will surely find it easier to prevent or cure leptin resistance. You can use this as an extensive guide to battle leptin resistance and prevent it from hampering the way you should live your life.

Chapter 1: What is Leptin and What Does it Do?

Also called the satiety hormone, leptin refers to a vital hormone produced by the adipose glands. Its main function is to regulate or control energy balance and fats by inhibiting hunger. Fat stores regulation is the primary function of leptin, but note that it also plays a number of physiological processes. Evidences of its effective physiological functions include the presence of multiple sites of synthesis aside from fat cells, and the different types of cells with leptin receptors aside from hypothalamic cells.

Leptin is closely linked to appetite and weight fluctuations. Produced naturally inside your body, it signals your brain when it is already full. However, there are certain factors that can disrupt or alter the balance of this hormone. These include two other hormones necessary in regulating appetite namely serotonin and insulin.

In case of weight gain, your leptin level will most likely rise, which will eventually cause your brain to transmit false hunger signals. This will further result to overeating. Leptin levels that go extremely beyond normal can also increase your risk of suffering from obesity and cardiovascular diseases. Studies show that maintaining the right balance or level of leptin requires making a few lifestyle changes while also balancing the intake of nutrients.

No one can underestimate the importance of leptin. Having the right level of this hormone will allow you to enjoy its numerous functions; one of which is its ability to work as an effective gatekeeper of fat metabolism. It also works in keeping track of the level of energy taken in by an organism. Another important function of leptin is that it retains the right energy balance of your body.

You can also expect it to regulate hunger with the aid of three pathways. One pathway is that it counteracts the effects stimulated by neuropeptide Y. This refers to a powerful feeding stimulant that specific gut cells as well as the hypothalamus secrete. The second pathway is that it counteracts the effects stimulated by anandamide, which is also a feeding stimulant. The third pathway used by leptin in regulating hunger is by stimulating a-MSH production, which refers to an appetite suppressant.

It is also crucial to note that the level of leptin released by fat cells depends upon the amount of fats your body has. If you have more fat stores, then expect it to cause the release of more leptin. Aside from the functions mentioned above, leptin also regulates your energy expenditure and metabolism. The right leptin level, one which is not too low nor too high, can also work effectively in improving your brain fitness and mental sharpness. This can also help improve your memory and your mood.

Chapter 2: Leptin Resistance: Its Causes

Leptin resistance refers to a condition characterized by the inability of your body to control appetite despite having high levels of the hormone. In other words, your body does not respond to leptin the way it supposed to even though you have more than enough of it. This causes you to gain weight even if you tried to maintain a healthy level of leptin.

The condition does not have a definitive cause yet, but certain factors and cellular mechanisms contribute to getting it. Two main hypothesis are also behind leptin resistance. The first hypothesis is that the leptin hormone found in the blood does not reach the right target to regulate appetite. The second one is that the receptors primarily bound by leptin tend to stop functioning correctly, thereby causing them to be unable to send a signal to your cells and brain to respond to the hormone.

The second scenario usually happens in both obese and overweight people, which makes it more difficult for them to prevent weight gain and control their appetite. The following are also some of the common triggers of leptin resistance.

Inflammation

One of the main factors that trigger leptin resistance is inflammation. According to studies conducted to both animal and human subjects, inflammatory signals to the hypothalamus can cause the body to resist the hormone.

Free Fatty Acids

High levels of free fatty acids in the bloodstream can also cause leptin resistance. The increased free fatty acids in your bloodstream can also raise the amount of fat metabolites in your brain. This can further interfere with the way leptin works.

Extremely High Leptin Levels

While maintaining sufficient amount of leptin in the body is important in maintaining a healthy weight and improving your health, an extremely high level of it (that which goes excessively beyond the normal levels) can also cause resistance. This is the main reason why you have to determine the specific amount of leptin that you need.

Other factors that contribute to leptin resistance are excessive consumption of fructose especially the high fructose corn syrup variety, too much consumption of simple carbs, inadequate sleep, high levels of stress, overeating, too much exercise, excessive consumption of leptin and grain and high insulin levels.

Chapter 3: What are the Symptoms of Leptin Resistance?

Learning about the major symptoms of leptin resistance is crucial in finding immediate cure for the condition. This chapter covers some of the common symptoms of the condition so you will know exactly what to watch out for and act on it right away.

Weight Gain

Leptin resistant sufferers are usually either overweight or obese. The main reason behind this is that the hormone no longer functions the way it supposed to. You will be at risk of gaining excess weight if you are already resistant to leptin since the hormone will no longer be able to help in regulating your appetite.

Increased cravings

Another of the most common symptoms of leptin resistance is increased cravings. You will also most likely feel hungry all the time, especially during odd hours (ex. at midnight). Note that the inability of your body to respond properly to leptin causes it be unable to control your appetite.

Your brain will not also receive the right signal. This means that even if you are already full, your brain will still think that you are hungry, thereby causing you to overeat. This further results to other symptoms that trigger sudden and uncontrollable weight gain such as increased cravings for high-calorie, comfort and fast foods, unusual eating patterns, huge appetite, overeating and increased cravings for carbohydrate-laden foods.

Difficulty losing weight

Leptin resistance also makes it hard for you to lose weight. You may be exercising too much, but you will still find it hard to lose weight considering the fact that your eating patterns will be drastically affected. You will also notice that your body stays the same no matter how long and frequent you perform your exercises.

The fact that you will be unable to control your appetite and cravings makes it hard for you to lose excess weight or maintain a healthy one. The only thing that you can do to start losing weight is to correct your leptin levels by making some changes in your diet and lifestyle.

Slow metabolism

Healthy leptin levels also play a crucial role in raising your metabolic rate. If your leptin level is either too high or too low, then your metabolism will also be drastically affected. It can cause your metabolism to slow down, which can also have a negative effect on your weight loss efforts. This problem can also lead to a number of other hormone-related conditions including thyroid problems, insulin resistance, low testosterone levels affecting males, Type 2 diabetes and PCOS (poly-cystic ovary syndrome).

Increased cholesterol level and high blood pressure

Another symptom of leptin resistance is the sudden increase in your cholesterol level and blood pressure. This is primarily because of your elevated triglycerides level. Note that too much triglycerides can greatly interfere with the functions of leptin to send the right signal to the brain. One way to prevent leptin resistance, and high cholesterol and blood pressure for that matter, is to try lowering your triglyceride levels.

Other Known Symptoms

Aside from the leptin resistance symptoms mentioned above, there are other signs that indicate that you already have the condition. Among these are disturbed or poor sleeping patterns, food sensitivities, high stress levels, mood swings, irritability, high blood sugar, allergies, fatigue, fatty liver, sugar cravings, urge to eat snacks even if you have just taken a big meal, and inability to lose weight despite regularly performing long and strenuous exercises.

If you put a check in most, if not all, of the symptoms mentioned in this chapter, then consider consulting medical experts. Find out if you really have leptin resistance so you can immediately correct the disorder.

Chapter 4: How do you know if you are resistant to Leptin?

If you suspect that you are resistant to leptin based on the symptoms mentioned in the previous chapter, then take note that you can undergo a few tests to determine if you really have it. This chapter covers some of these tests.

Check for physical symptoms

One of the fastest ways to determine if you are leptin resistant is to check whether you have the physical symptoms of the condition. The first thing that you should check is your weight. Note that the specific location of your excess body fats and the amount of excess weight are indicators of the condition. Note that just like diabetes sufferers, leptin resistance patients also tend to gain excess weight rapidly in the middle. They also have high levels of excess body fats.

You also need to check your sleeping patterns and habits. Note that insomnia, unhealthy sleeping patterns and fatigue are among the common signs of the condition. Another physical symptom that you need to check is your blood pressure. You most likely have leptin resistance if your blood pressure reading is more than 130/85.

The current condition of your skin also indicates whether you have leptin resistance. Check your skin and find out if you have stretch marks, skin tags or skin darkening or discoloration visible around the skin folds, the armpits and neck. Note that these are among the most commonly missed indicators of the condition.

You can also consult your doctor regarding PCOS (polycystic ovary syndrome). PCOS symptoms usually include fertility problems, acne, abnormal menstrual cycles and facial hair growth, all of which are among the common physical signs of leptin resistance.

Blood Sugar Level

One way to determine if you are resistant to leptin is to measure your blood sugar level. Do it after fasting for at least 12 hours. A wise tip is to do it in the morning. You are most likely resistant to leptin if your regular morning blood sugar reading is more than 95 mg/dL. You can also take the AC1 test in a clinic. AC1 refers to a person's 3-month average blood sugar level. A test result of more than 5.6 AC1 is indicative of leptin resistance.

C-reactive Protein (CRP), Homocysteine and PAI-1 (Plasminogen Activator Inhibitor) Test

The results of these three tests can also help you determine if you are already resistant to leptin. CRP is a reliable test because it helps in measuring inflammation, which is one of the symptoms of the condition. Homocysteine tests are also essential in determining cardiovascular diseases and blood clots that can greatly affect your leptin levels. PAI-1 refers to a fat cell protein which is also capable of increasing your risk of dealing with cardiovascular diseases and blood clots. This can further lead to leptin resistance.

Leptin Test

While the usefulness of leptin test is yet to be established, some of those who undergo it say that they were able to determine whether they are resistant to leptin successfully. In a clinical setting, the test is usually conducted to an overweight or obese person especially if he/she shows symptoms of persistent and frequent hunger. The test is essential in detecting whether the patient has leptin deficiency or if he has excessive amounts of it.

To produce more accurate results, the test is usually conducted with other examinations like insulin, glucose, thyroid panel and lipid profile. The combined tests are necessary to check the current health condition of an overweight or obese person and to determine whether there is an underlying condition that complicates or worsens lipid resistance.

Measuring your triglycerides and cholesterol levels, as well as blood pressure can also help. You can also have your thyroid hormone tested. Note that thyroid issues are also often linked to leptin, so it is crucial to have yours tested. With the help of the tests mentioned in this chapter, you will be on your way towards confirming whether you have the condition.

Chapter 5: Overcoming Leptin Resistance with Diet Changes

If you have leptin resistance, then rest assured that it is not yet the end of the weight loss journey for you. You can still overcome the condition and maintain a better and healthy weight by just performing a few dietary changes. Just take note of a few vital rules when it comes to the leptin diet.

Avoid eating after dinner

Are you one of those who enjoy eating midnight snacks? Do you feel the need to eat a second dinner as a means to relieve stress or relax? If your answer is yes to both questions, then you are at risk of ruining your weight loss efforts. Your weight will further increase especially if you have leptin resistance. Eating after dinner will also cause you to gain even more weight since it counteracts the diet plan and the workout routines that you are currently following.

The truth is the later you eat, the higher the chance that the foods consumed will get stored as excess fats in your body, instead of being converted to energy. This scenario is further aggravated by the fact that the current leptin level in your body does not work as it should. Try to limit the foods that you eat at night. Focus on the bare minimum and eat it three hours before going to sleep. This can help a lot if you are suffering from leptin resistance.

Take three meals daily

Make sure that you still get the three required meals in a day. The best way to do this is to maintain a 3 to 6-hour gap in between each meal, and avoid snacking. Take note that unhealthy snacking and consuming small meals between your breakfast, lunch and dinner are among the things that can make you lose track of the foods you consume.

You may even think that you are eating lesser amount of calories than you actually do. This kind of mindset can only lead to frustration in the end, especially if your goal is to become skinny. One way to avoid snacking in between your three daily meals is to drink a lot. Hydrate with pure water, not with coffee or diet sodas, since the latter may only cause you to become hungrier than what you actually feel.

Some people also often think that they are hungry when in fact what they are feeling is thirst. If you are leptin resistant, then it pays to increase your water intake since this can prevent you from overeating.

Avoid consuming huge meals

Practice portion eating, especially if your body's resistance to leptin is already taking a toll on your overall weight and health. If you are already overweight, then the best way to avoid consuming a huge meal is to stop whenever you feel that you are slightly full. Note that it usually takes around ten to twenty minutes for your brain to receive the signal that your stomach is already full.

Another tip is to eat slowly. You should also learn to listen to your internal cue, so you will know exactly when to stop. You have to start practicing the habit of mindful eating since this can help a lot in your attempt to stop overeating. You also need to remind yourself that eating huge portions can mess up the process of creating the right amount of leptin in your body.

This will prevent the formation of the hormone and its proper function once you start the habit of eating smaller meals. This can further lead to increased leptin resistance, thereby lengthening the amount of time that it usually takes for you to feel full and satisfied.

Add protein-rich foods to your breakfast

If you want to maintain healthy leptin levels, then it is advisable to focus more on eating a healthy breakfast. Add protein-rich foods to your breakfast since protein can benefit those who are resistant to the hormone. Eating a protein-rich breakfast also helps prevent unwanted cravings and hunger.

You can also raise your metabolism by up to thirty percent for twelve long hours by consuming a high-protein breakfast. This type of breakfast proves to be extremely useful for leptin resistance sufferers who struggle in maintaining a healthy weight. With the help of protein, you can avoid dealing with low energy, unhealthy food cravings, and increased body weight that are the usual leptin resistance symptoms.

Reduce your overall carbohydrate consumption

Carbohydrate-rich foods such as pastries, ice cream and bread are among the tastiest foods in the planet. However, these are also the worst enemies of people who are resistant to leptin since excessive carb intake can ruin your weight loss efforts. Just remember that you do not need to get rid of carbs completely from your diet. Note that you still need it for the proper functioning of your thyroid.

Lack of carb can also cause your muscles to weaken, the inability of your body to burn fats efficiently and prevent your growth hormones from being released the right way. This is the main reason why many leptin diet experts do not recommend a no-carb diet. The key here is to limit your carb consumption. If you are leptin resistant, then the best way to limit your carb intake is to get it from healthy sources like fruits, vegetables, yogurt, small amount of butter and cottage cheese.

Sample Meal Plan for a Leptin Diet

This sample meal plan for leptin resistance sufferers will serve as your guide in preparing your own.

Breakfast - Because your condition requires you to eat a high-protein breakfast, you need to eat foods that are considered to be healthy sources of the nutrient. Among the protein-rich foods that you can include in your breakfast are protein shakes, pork chops, steak and eggs.

Lunch - You may have a hard time preparing your lunch especially if you feel really hungry. The key is to include a number of foods with low calories in your lunch. Among your best choices would be a soup, salad, boiled meat such as turkey or chicken and unsweetened tea such as black and green tea.

Dinner - You should keep your dinner preparation simple. A wise tip is to go for small servings of vegetables, protein-rich foods and fruits. You can also eat whip cream or ice cream, as long as you keep the servings to the bare minimum. Make sure that your dinner is the smallest meal of the three.

You can also incorporate healthy superfoods in any of your meals. Some superfoods work in balancing your leptin levels while also jump-starting your healthy eating habits. Among the superfoods that you can include in your meals are Romaine lettuce, flaxseed, basil, bell pepper, vegetable juice, green tea, blueberry juice, broccoli, cabbage carrots, walnuts, cherries, grapefruit and apples.

Foods to Avoid

You also need to avoid certain foods if you do not want to aggravate your condition. Your leptin resistance requires you to stay away from processed carbohydrates, particularly those that are rich in flour and sugar. You should also eliminate fatty cuts of meat from your diet. Foods that cause inflammation can also trigger the aggravation of your condition.

Among the inflammatory foods that you should consider avoiding include conventional processed foods like breakfast cereals, bagels, burgers, pizza, French fries, packed granola bars, sodas, low-fat milk, conventional ice cream and chicken nuggets. You should also be willing to let go of any processed or fast food.

Chapter 6: Managing Leptin Resistance with Supplements

Managing leptin resistance is possible by taking the right supplements. This chapter will cover some of the most valuable supplements that you can take to deal with the condition.

Fucoxanthin

Fucoxanthin refers to a dietary supplement based on a carotenoid naturally present in brown seaweed. According to studies, it has an anti-obesity effect, so it helps a lot for those who have a hard time managing their weight due to leptin resistance. It also promotes healthy inflammation, thereby allowing those who take it to fight their resistance from leptin.

Zinc

Taking a zinc supplement can also help you a lot if you are resistant to leptin. Both leptin and zinc can promote a healthy immune system. Both can also influence the amount of foods that you consume. Zinc ensures that your body has a healthy supply of leptin, while the latter works in managing your weight. Zinc also aids in bolstering the ability of the hormone to perform its optimal functions.

The good thing about zinc supplements is that they are available in various forms. You can take this supplement to deal with leptin resistance, but make sure that your dosage does not exceed 40 milligrams daily.

Irvingia Gabonensis

Irvingia gabonensis holds the most promise when it comes to reversing leptin resistance. Also known as African mango extract, Irvingia gabonensis extract can help those who are leptin resistant lose weight by blocking new fat deposition, absorbing sugar and acting as a safe laxative. It also helps ensure that your leptin is at a healthy level. Studies show that this supplement is capable of lowering an excessively high leptin level, thereby supporting weight loss.

The ability of the supplement to decrease C-reactive protein in your fat cells can also help reverse leptin resistance in the brain. This allows you to bring back the normal levels of leptin in your body, which is a huge help in managing weight and preventing the consumption of excess calories. The supplement can also lower inflammation, which is one of the most uncomfortable and devastating symptoms of the condition.

Omega-3 Fatty Acids

Another supplement that you should consider taking if you have leptin resistance is Omega-3. This supplement plays a crucial role in maintaining healthy levels of leptin and in fighting inflammation. If you have the condition and you want to fight it through Omega-3 fatty acids supplement, then take note that the safest dosage for you is 3mg. Avoid exceeding that dosage to get the maximum benefits of the supplement without harming yourself.

Supplements designed to reverse and fight the symptoms of leptin resistance is crucial in maintaining good health and in losing weight. The right leptin supplement for you can help a lot in regulating your appetite. The supplement is extremely helpful for those who plan to lose weight and those who already feel lethargic due to the condition.

Chapter 7: Optimizing Exercise for Leptin Resistance

Performing regular exercises is extremely useful in beating leptin resistance. Your regular workout is even more useful if you have already become overweight and obese due to your condition. Exercise also has a strong influence in maintaining healthy levels of hormones in your body, leptin included. It has a positive effect on leptin resistance patients. Even moderate exercises are enough to help the hormone function better, thereby preventing you from gaining weight and reducing your cravings and appetite.

High Intensity Exercises

High intensity exercises work effectively for those who are leptin resistant. One example of this workout is the popular high intensity interval training (HIIT). This workout works in stimulating huge secretions of HGH (human growth hormone) that can result to a bolstered fat burning mechanism. This can further regulate the level of leptin inside your body.

High intensity workouts combined with weight lifting can also do a lot of good when it comes to fighting leptin resistance. This can beat the condition without putting a lot of stress to your body. Experts suggest performing these types of workout in the evening, instead of in the morning, since this move can stimulate healthy hormone levels.

Aerobic Exercises

Aerobic exercise is also good for leptin resistance patients. It is one of the best fat burning exercises, especially if you have already reached that level of fitness that allows you to perform it for more than an hour. However, take note that stretching, general physical activities, walking and strength training are equally important as aerobics. Regularly performing aerobic exercises also aids in curbing your appetite. It boosts brain rejuvenation while also suppressing your appetite.

Aerobic exercise also raises the number of active leptin receptors within your body, which makes it possible for the hormone to perform its functions optimally especially in terms of regulating your weight. This form of exercise can also help a lot in detoxifying your body, thereby getting rid of harmful toxins. This means that you do not only burn calories; you also get rid of the bad stuff inside your body.

If you run regularly as a means of fulfilling your aerobic workouts, then expect your leptin to function a lot better. Running makes it possible for the hormone to turn on the system in your muscles that is responsible in disposing calories as heat. This is possible through the activation of the process called uncoupling muscle protein.

You can also simply start your regular physical activities by adhering to a walking program that comes with intervals. This is usually enough to kick-start your leptin and allow it to function properly. Once you get used to performing regular exercises, start focusing on weight lifting and high intensity workouts.

Note that these exercises can beat the negative effects of leptin resistance by allowing you to lose weight and building leaner muscles. This can further result to a firmer and more trimmed body. Once your leptin hormone starts to operate more efficiently with proper exercises, you can expect to enjoy its benefits again including a well-regulated appetite and higher energy.

Chapter 8: Alternative Medicines for Leptin Resistance

Leptin resistance is also curable through alternative medicines. These include natural treatments and practices including meditation, reflexology, massage and acupuncture. This chapter will focus on providing brief information about these alternative medicines and how these can help in beating leptin resistance.

Meditation

Meditation refers to a popular practice which involves focusing or concentrating on a specific thing; for instance, your breathing. It is effective in relieving stress. It stimulates focus and concentration, which aids in promoting relaxation. Note that excessive stress can have a negative impact on your hormones, leptin included. It can trigger hormone imbalance.

With the help of meditation, you get to relax your body and mind, which is a major help in regulating leptin. It also addresses any imbalance found in your hypothalamus-pituitary pathways, so regulating your hormones will no longer become that hard.

Reflexology

The core of reflexology is vitalism, a popular concept that explains that an innate intelligence governs the human body. This innate intelligence promotes self-healing. If you have leptin resistance, then reflexology can help you a lot by stimulating the self-healing process. It also reduces your stress levels, making it possible for you to bring back the balance of the most important hormones in your body including leptin.

Reflexology also deals with inflammation, one of the most common symptoms of leptin resistance. Aside from reversing leptin resistance, reflexology also promotes better health by relieving anxiety, preventing headache pain, fighting Type 2 diabetes, promoting better heart health and fighting cancer.

Acupuncture

Acupuncture can also offer numerous benefits to those who are suffering from leptin resistance. This alternative medicine has long been recognized for its weight loss effects. The good thing about acupuncture is that it uses your hormonal system as a means of changing your hunger drives and increasing your satiety. This alternative medicine also uses your acupuncture points to manipulate ghrelin and leptin, the most vital hormones responsible in regulating appetite and body weight.

Those who regularly undergo acupuncture sessions also reported reduced leptin resistance and insulin levels, which results to weight loss.

Massage

Getting a regular massage can also help a lot when it comes to correcting leptin resistance. It promotes relaxation and improves mood, both benefits are also good in maintaining healthy levels of leptin. It also offers an aid in controlling your appetite. The fact that it relieves stress is also an indication that it supports the functions of your body and promotes the right balance of hormones. Regular massage can also help regulate your sleeping patterns and improve the quality of your sleep, which is beneficial in correcting leptin imbalance.

Essential Oils

If you have leptin resistance and you find it really hard to lose weight because of the condition, then note that there are essential oils that aid in managing the condition. Most essential oils aid in weight loss because of their ability to cure cravings, improve digestion and promote a healthy metabolism. One essential oil that can help you in this area is grapefruit. Aside from reducing cravings, grapefruit essential oil can also lower insulin and leptin levels, which is beneficial in regulating blood sugar, fat storage and metabolism.

There is also an essential oil based on ginger. The fact that ginger is highly anti-inflammatory makes the essential oil capable of fighting the main symptom of leptin resistance which is inflammation. You can also use peppermint essential oil which is good in alleviating nausea, bloating and constipation.

Chapter 9: How to Deal with Congenital Leptin Resistance?

Congenital leptin resistance refers to a condition characterized by severe cases of obesity even during the first few months of a person's life. Those who suffer from it have normal weight at birth. However, they feel constant hunger, causing them to gain weight quickly. Without applying the right treatment, the child may experience extreme hunger continuously, which will eventually lead to severe excessive eating and obesity.

Because the condition starts during early childhood, it is no longer surprising for those who are affected by it to develop abnormal eating patterns and behaviors including eating in secret, hoarding foods and fighting over food. If you are a parent of a child with congenital leptin resistance, then do not lose hope since there are some things that you can do to manage the condition. One of the things that you can do is to always seek the advice of medical professionals.

Ask them about the possible treatments that you can use or if the current treatment plan followed by your child needs to be changed. You may also consider trying recombinant leptin. Treatments for leptin resistance that involve the use of recombinant leptin were reported to sustain weight reduction.

One study even indicated that the weight loss during the process of applying the treatment indicated a negative energy balance of around 400 kcal daily, on average. The treatment can also trigger a reduced basal metabolic rate, but this reduction is counterbalanced by increased energy expenditure attributed to physical activities.

As a parent, you also need to ensure that the foods eaten by a child with congenital leptin resistance are good for him. Start creating a leptin-friendly diet. Congenital leptin resistance sufferers may feel hungry most of the time, but you can help manage their weight by ensuring that the foods you feed them will not significantly increase their weight. You can consult the chapter that talked about diet and foods in this book to give you a clue on what to feed a congenital leptin resistance patient.

Also, it pays to engage your child in physical activities. You can develop a fitness or exercise program for him that is good for children. It does not have to be as arduous as the exercises performed by adults. Make it fun to keep him interested in the activity. You can let him play the sports that he loves. As long as you keep him moving, you have an assurance that some of the calories that he gets from the foods he eats are burned.

Chapter 10: Suggested Recipes for Changing your Diet

Making some dietary changes is crucial in correcting any imbalance in your hormones. This especially holds true if you have leptin resistance. The good news is that you do not have to force yourself to eat bland foods just to stick to a healthy diet plan and lose weight if you are leptin resistant. There are actually a lot of tasty recipes that can help correct any imbalance in your leptin levels. Some of these recipes are covered in this chapter.

Steak Burritos

This tasty recipe makes four servings. You can prepare it within just 45 minutes plus the 24-hour marinade. Prepare the following ingredients to get started.

For the marinade, you will need:

2 diced and seeded jalapenos

1 teaspoon salt

A bunch of cilantro leaves and stems

¼ cup toasted cumin seeds

½ cup lime juice

1 crushed garlic clove

1 tablespoon black pepper (cracked)

¾ cup olive oil

For the burrito, you will need:

Half cup of water

Half cup fresh salsa

¼ cup long grain brown rice (uncooked)

2 tablespoons fresh cilantro (coarsely chopped)

¼ cup guacamole (make sure that it is fresh)

1 can organic black beans (15-ounce can)

Half cup sharp cheddar cheese (shredded)

1 tablespoon olive oil

4 pieces 8-inch brown rice or whole-wheat tortillas

12-ounce thinly sliced and trimmed grass-fed strip steak

Procedure:

For the marinade, the first step is to place all the marinade ingredients in your blender. Blend the mixture until a smooth consistency is achieved. Pour the blended mixture over the slices of beef. Cover it and store in your refrigerator. Marinade overnight.

The next step is to cook the rice based on package directions. Add water and salsa to the rice ten minutes before completing the cooking time. Simmer for around five minutes. Add the beans. Simmer the mixture without cover until the rice becomes tender. This should take an additional five minutes.

Prepare a large skillet. Heat it over medium-high heat. Stir in steak slices. Cook the mixture while stirring occasionally. Continue cooking for three to five minutes or until the steaks turn brown.

Once done, you can start assembling them. You can do so by dividing the steaks among the tortillas. Use guacamole, cheese, rice mixture and cilantro as toppings. You can then roll the tortillas to make burritos.

Overnight Raspberry Vanilla Oatmeal

This recipe is ideal for leptin resistance sufferers who want easy to prepare meals that can provide them with the energy that they need in the morning. You can prepare this recipe by gathering the following ingredients:

¾ cup oats (uncooked)

Half scoop of wellness resources

Half cup almond milk

Salt

Half teaspoon vanilla extract

1 tablespoon date paste

Water

Procedure:

Mix all of the mentioned ingredients in a bowl. Store the mixture in your refrigerator and leave it overnight. You can then eat it for breakfast the following morning. Serve this recipe while cold along with fresh raspberries and sliced almonds.

Caprese Quinoa Salad

For this particular recipe, you will need the following ingredients:

Chopped fresh basil

Half cup organic quinoa

Kosher salt

2 tablespoons extra virgin olive oil

Pepper

8 ounce fresh mozzarella

1 box halved organic grape tomatoes

Procedure:

Boil 1 cup filtered water in medium pan. Add quinoa to the boiling water, then reduce heat. Simmer it for around fifteen minutes on low heat. Once done, remove the quinoa from heat and let it cool in your refrigerator for approximately one hour.

Cut the grape tomatoes in halves and the mozzarella into bite-sized pieces. Mix the two ingredients. You can then add them to the cooked and cooled quinoa. Mix well.

The next step is to drizzle olive oil over the salad. Add salt and pepper then serve.

Grilled Salmon and Rosemary Skewers

This leptin resistance recipe can make four servings. Here are the ingredients that you need:

2 minced garlic cloves

2 teaspoons fresh rosemary (minced)

1 teaspoon lemon juice

2 teaspoons extra virgin olive oil

1 pint cherry tomatoes

¼ teaspoon pepper (freshly ground)

1 teaspoon lemon zest (freshly grated)

1 pound wild salmon fillet - Look for the center-cut variety, remove the skin and cut it into cubes around 1 inch

Half teaspoon kosher salt

Procedure:

Preheat your grill using medium high heat. Prepare a medium bowl and mix oil, lemon juice and zest, garlic, rosemary, salt and pepper there. Add salmon into the bowl. Toss everything to coat.

Once done, you can divide the mixture among eight skewers. Make sure to alternate the tomatoes and salmon.

The next step is to add some oil on your grill rack. Start grilling the skewers. Turn once carefully and wait for around four to six minutes. Serve this dish right away.

Chicken Kabobs

Ingredients:

Freshly squeezed juice of one lime

Cilantro

1 teaspoon garlic (minced)

3 tablespoons tamari

4 organic chicken breast halves (boneless and skinless)

1 tablespoon extra virgin olive oil

Procedure:

Get a small bowl so you can start mixing the extra virgin olive oil, tamari, cilantro, garlic and lime juice. The next step is to cut the chicken breasts into large chunks. Skewer them into bamboo sticks soaked in water for around five minutes. Marinade for a minimum of thirty minutes.

Once done, you can grill the chicken using medium high setting. Do this for around six to eight minutes per side. Serve this dish right away with steamed vegetables or fresh salad.

The recipes above are just five of the many healthy and tasty recipes for leptin resistance sufferers. While you need to make some changes in your diet so you can finally lose weight, rest assured that it does not mean that you should eat bland and tasteless foods. The recipes mentioned above are proof that you can still lose weight while eating healthy and delicious foods even if you are leptin resistant.

Chapter 11: The Leptin Resistance Cheat Sheet

To help you in your journey towards treating leptin resistance, this chapter will compile some of the do's and don'ts provided by this book so far. This will serve as a recap of all the information that this book has provided. Consult this leptin resistance cheat sheet from time to time, so you will have an easier time managing and beating the symptoms of the condition.

Do's

Learn more about the symptoms and causes of the condition, so you will know exactly how to deal with it.

Check for physical symptoms.

Undergo certain tests that will help you determine whether you are resistant to leptin. Some of the tests that you can undergo include blood sugar test, C-reactive protein (CRP), Homocysteine and PAI-1 (Plasminogen Activator Inhibitor) tests and leptin test.

Eat three meals in a day.

Add protein-rich foods to your breakfast.

Take supplements that will help manage leptin resistance symptoms including fucoxanthin, zinc, irvingia gabonensis and Omega-3.

Perform regular exercises especially aerobic and high intensity interval training.

Try alternative medicines. These include meditation, acupuncture, reflexology, massage and the application of essential oils.

Don'ts

Eat snacks frequently - If you are leptin resistant, you need to avoid snacking as much as possible. Focus on getting your daily nutritional requirement from your three main meals: breakfast, lunch and dinner.

Eat huge meals - You only need to eat three main meals a day, but that does not mean that you should fill each one with too much foods. It is crucial to put some limits in your meals. Know exactly what is enough for your body. It helps to eat slowly since it often takes 15-20 minutes for your body to recognize that you are already full.

Eat after dinner - Eating after dinner, for instance during midnight, can only sabotage your weight loss efforts. Note that the foods you eat after dinner will only get stored in your body as excess fats. If possible, limit your food intake at dinner, as well.

Eat carbohydrate-rich foods - Your current condition requires you to stay away from foods laden with unhealthy carbohydrates. These include processed carbohydrates from food products rich in flour and sugar.

Eat fatty cuts of meat - If you want to beat leptin resistance, then avoiding fatty substances is also one of the things that you should do. These include fatty cuts of meat.

Eat inflammatory foods - Note that inflammation is one of the primary symptoms of leptin resistance. If you eat inflammatory foods, then you will only aggravate your condition. Some of the inflammatory foods that you need to eliminate from your diet are processed foods, packed granola bars and chicken nuggets.

By keeping in mind the mentioned do's and don'ts, you will be on your way towards managing leptin resistance and bringing back your once healthy weight.

Chapter 12: Further Online Resources and Tools

Overcoming leptin resistance is all about having all the information that you need about the condition. The good news is that you can find more about the condition through a number of online resources. One of the most reliable online source of information regarding leptin resistance is wellnessresources.com. It provides numerous facts about health and wellness including leptin resistance, possible solutions to the condition and developing the best leptin diet.

You can also seek the aid of other online resources where you can find most information regarding various health conditions. These include webmd.com and livestrong.com. Aside from all the valuable information that you will get from the mentioned resources, you can also beat leptin resistance with the additional tips mentioned in this chapter.

Make fish a part of your weekly meal plans

Based on the study made by the American Heart Association in 2002, weekly meal plans containing fish can help in lowering or regulating leptin levels. Consider eating mackerel, tuna and salmon at least two times per week to regulate the hormone. The best methods of cooking fish include grilling and baking. Avoid fried fish because this contains high fat content. You may also choose to take fish oil supplements. Just make sure to ask the advice of your doctor before taking the supplement to guarantee your safety.

Don't forget to add a re-feed day or cheat meal

This is extremely useful especially once you feel that your metabolism starts to slow down. A re-feed day mainly consists of 20-50 percent increase in the calorie level that you normally maintain. One tip in ensuring that you get the most out of your re-feed day is to raise your carbohydrate intake by 100-150 percent during this day. Your re-feed or cheat day can help in jump-starting your metabolism while also normalizing your leptin levels. Just make sure that you do not do this too often.

Get enough sleep

Some studies show that those who experience problems getting the recommended number of hours of sleep per night have leptin levels that are 15 percent lower than those who have adequate sleep. The main reason behind this is that the hormone usually increases or functions at its best during sleep cycle. With this in mind, it is safe to conclude that getting adequate sleep is crucial in beating leptin resistance. The good thing about having 8 hours of sleep is that this can also control your appetite.

Good quality sleep also contributes to the proper functioning of leptin. Note that sleep disorders and deprivation can trigger leptin resistance, which further results to lower metabolism, increased and uncontrollable appetite, diabetes and other ailments.

Reduce the amount of triglyceride in your body

High blood triglycerides level can inhibit the proper transmission of leptin from your blood to your brain. This is the main reason why you have to work hard in reducing your triglyceride level if you want to regulate your leptin hormone. One solution when it comes to lowering triglycerides level is to reduce your intake of carb-rich foods.

Eat green vegetables in the morning

If possible, do this tip before ten in the morning. Make it a habit to include green vegetables in your morning meal plans or daily breakfast since this can help a lot in curing leptin resistance. The good thing about these vegetables is that these serve as effective vitamin supplements that nourish your body.

Reduce inflammation

The presence of excess fats in your body can trigger inflammation. Excess fat cells produce inflammatory chemicals called cytokines that can cause a lot of damage to your body. Try to reduce your weight so you can lower inflammation. You should also stay away from inflammatory foods to avoid inflammation that can aggravate your resistance to leptin.

Conclusion

Thank you again for downloading this book!

I hope this book was able to help you learn more about leptin resistance and how it can put your health and your entire body in danger. Leptin resistance is one of the most common causes of weight problems. Your inability to respond well to leptin can cause you to suffer from a number of weight-related problems including obesity.

The good news is that there are numerous ways to deal with the condition. Some of these solutions are offered in this book. The next step is to follow all the tips and solutions for leptin resistance found in this book. You will surely notice a significant improvement in your leptin levels by following the tips that you can find here. Start to bring back the right balance of leptin in your body and enjoy an improved health and a healthier weight.

Finally, if you enjoyed this book, please take the time to share your thoughts and post a review on Amazon. It'd be greatly appreciated!

Thank you and good luck!

Made in the USA
Middletown, DE
05 December 2015